THE FAST HEAT OF BEAUTY

For my parents

THE FAST HEAT OF BEAUTY

Anna McKerrow

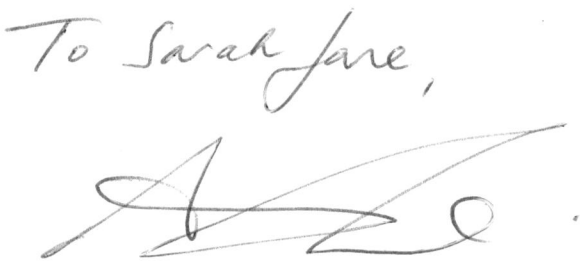

First published in Great Britain in 2008 by Flambard Press
Stable Cottage, East Fourstones, Hexham NE47 5DX
www.flambardpress.co.uk

Typeset by BookType
Cover design by Gainford Design Associates and Johanna Ward
Cover and author photographs by Johanna Ward
Printed in Great Britain by Cromwell Press, Trowbridge, Wiltshire

A CIP catalogue record for this book
is available from the British Library.
ISBN 978-1-873226-96-4

Copyright © Anna McKerrow 2008
All rights reserved.
Anna McKerrow has exerted her moral rights in accordance
with the Copyright, Designs and Patents Act of 1988.

Flambard Press wishes to thank Arts Council England
for its financial support.

Flambard Press is a member of Inpress,
and of Independent Northern Publishers.

Acknowledgements

'The Doctor' originally appeared as 'The Healer' in *Cadenza*; 'The Luxuries of the Desired Are Dreams' originally appeared in *Orbis Quarterly International Literary Journal*; 'Unseasonal' originally appeared in *Sentinel Poetry Quarterly*; 'China Doll' originally appeared in *Obsessed with Pipework*; 'Aphrodite' and 'Between Boaz and Joachim' originally appeared in *The Dawntreader*; 'Creatrix' and 'Networking' originally appeared in *Crannog*.

Contents

The Fast Heat of Beauty	9
Lot's Wife	10
The Way Men Hold Their Heads	11
This Is a Fist	12
Eulogy	13
The Luxuries of the Desired Are Dreams	14
You Write Her Name on You	15
Occasional Lover	16
Waiting	17
The Serpent Temple	18
Man	19
What We Refused to Bring to Birth	20
Narcissus Road	21
An Unquiet Love	22
Nullity	23
Quietly Observing Him	24
This Is Me For You	25
Love Is Suffering's Reward	26
Healing	27
Making Potions	28
Mythologies	29
Yesodic	30
Between Boaz and Joachim	31
O Beautiful Lord	32
Turkish Bath	33
Aphrodite	34
Sea Mysteries	35
Dream	36
Good Faith	38

Artist	39
Networking	40
The Doctor	41
Patchwork and Hope	42
Visionary	43
Fairylight	44
It Was Nearly a Baby	45
Jeans for Thoughtful Girls	46
Creatrix	47
Quiet	48
It's War	49
If Words Were Paint	50
China Doll	51
We Are Innocents	52
Unseasonal	53
Soft Roads Lead Home	54
Vanda	55
Sitwellian Ego Dramas	56
Tears Will Get You in the End	57
Teignmouth	58
Outline	59
Centre of the Line	60
Body	61
The Nucleus of Creation	62
Justine, Office Slut	63
In Response to a Piece of Performance Art	64

The Fast Heat of Beauty

Build the temple. The thousands will come;
they will break its walls with their singing.

Like glass that shatters at true pitch, they will vaporise
the cloudiness that shrouds them.

There will be nothing but air, held together with
bright, far-reaching brilliance, permeating
the true-hearted masses,

where the only shrine is the fast heat of beauty,
real and raw and uncorrupted.

Lot's Wife

You looked back at what was bigger than you,
a whole city in flames, and you risked it, your name,
your father-given name,
to see fire consume sin. And then, to join the far-off sea,
you were salt, waiting for the water rushing in.

We remember you, victim of a cautionary tale.
That Woman came and saw, was tempted and fell.
Isn't that how it goes, how men wrote it?
That lust was your tell, and what womankind brought:

everyone looked – you just got caught.

The Way Men Hold Their Heads

The way men hold their heads –
slightly cocked, waiting for trees to fall,
or piles of lumber to construct themselves
from the force of their own thrust.

All rush and assurance in that kink,
saying, 'World, female:
I am poised, deadly,
the inevitable fist from the shoulder,'
calling dull orange, brick-red energy,
hard light to swirl in eddies
in a fast, compact discus –
Atlas, ready to chuck.

This Is a Fist

This is a fist: sisters,
preserve your kisses,
charge into oblivion with surrendered cries.
Learn to love the murderous look in his eyes.
This is a fist: the force no woman can resist.

Eulogy

What a year it's been.
A whole year between us,
a whole year it's been.

I must be a little advanced, as karma
has had its revenge right back
and hit me, smack! Deservedly
and with no warning, a guerrilla attack.

Only twelve months since we chanced our luck on nothing,
a sure bet that a future without each other
would be a better future yet.

What a year, what changes:
I'm smaller, you're rich.
Next time I'll choose someone taller.
You'll go for less of a bitch.

A woman who'll believe in your hygienic classless dreams.
You could have babies and be a stay-at-home dad.
In that case she'd be a career woman, though – too bad.
She'd be on your case around the clock for your
lazy chaos and your eternal dirty socks.

And all the time with the kids
sprouting up like mushrooms in the night.
In your mind you're re-cleaving the world in two
but doing it right:
no class, no colour, and
no passion, no magic, no fight.

The Luxuries of the Desired Are Dreams

The luxuries of the desired are dreams,
green-wash scenes on a half-eye, and
fancy turns him this way, and that;

and to watch him dream, when drones
spell out Palladian texts on his Grecian brow,
the day in half a cup, and his
long-limbed slumber, thumbs turned in,
no air for the crash and conflict of men now.

When that knotted rope,
hemp and twine and song and sound,
when it pulls him under, I am wakeful,
marshalling painted processions that tramp past on borrowed steam.

The dreams of the desired are an easy lull –
so let him sleep, in purgatory, for now.

You Write Her Name on You

Write on your hand, rehearse her name.
You trace it over, write it again.
Is it so beautiful? Endemic, inked into you, a brand.
Blueball her name on one backhand.

Before you were a man, before
you dreamed, you clocked UFOs on grey nights,
you adventured, you set your sights
on higher realms. You were all
celestial, heaven and hell.
Before, you lay on your back and kicked.

Now, you slump, whipped,
and her name is written on your hands, on your
broad back, your thighs;
colonised your strength, she has,
she has conquered enemy lands.
Her love devours, marks flesh as its own.

That swampy brand, that jungle smell she sows under your skin;
and you have forgotten everything of me now, almost everything.

Occasional Lover

I know you know I'm looking.
You can feel my look, ripping
your top buttons off, my thumb in your mouth;
latitude and languorous plans are not ours,
we live minutes hand to mouth;
no breadth, no depth: no flow,
more a colliding of power –
and it's just some of you, no time for all, just some,
and that time is rushed and rough;
but you're enough, occasional lover; enough.

Waiting

Chaotic and sweet it is, to wait for you.
When eyes within eyes flick at a purged city;
only exhaustion closes them, on
late movies in which only you star.

I wait for you to dawn, for your godly glow
to send the shadows packing,
to bleach out my night mysteries.

You arrive new every day, fresh with daylight mischief.

The Serpent Temple

I will raise the serpent temple to you –
this is to what it has come;
black magic, control of the disincarnate, voodoo.
You have made my eyes dim, smudged, black.
Retaliation, revenge: I am taking you back.

There is no will that can withstand mine.
There will be no resistance, no time,
no time to wander and roam.

I take the amber pillars, the green stalks, and
raise the serpent temple so he walks
with me in its darkness, in the shroud.

I will raise the snakes for him,
crossed over my head, and live under their bite.

And there will be no love.
And there will be no light, no grace.
There will only be my victory, my prize,
my eyes dim, smudged, black.
Retaliation, revenge: I have taken you back.

Man

A new bitter blood taste of alpha,
competition, cordite and strong arms –
your thick copper haze of male
corresponds to a twitching hormone response;
and I am all woman again,
blue heather honey and self-conscious, pouty mouth.

What We Refused to Bring to Birth

What we refused to bring to birth,
what we could never keep alive between us was
understanding: your tie tied me, my feet, and
my nylons gagged you, your mouth,
domestic materials kept in the torturer's cupboard, by the gas
    meter, on the stairs.

We drew them out, practised on each other until
one was muffled and one could neither run nor fly.

We had to do it
together, contort ourselves and make a private hell
in a maisonette;
I guess to learn,
to rub the edges off with wire wool, glasspaper,
to bleach our love out with sugar soap,
to evolve, to turn, to turn.

Narcissus Road

Narcissus Road, my old view,
my potted history of regrets.
Most of all I attribute to you
not enough hot sex.

An Unquiet Love

A quiet moment, late, looking at your window, looking
at an unquiet love. A new old love,
unexplained, from another time,
dismembered and reattached;
not fully prescient, but not wanting you less –
love shadows heavy on the breath and out-breath,

and it is meant. Breath, stopped, held,
my feet, my hands. Bound, kept for you.
This quiet maroon, deep blue – this silent shell,
cupping chaos, guarding you from harm,
from a very uncertain hell.

It must break; the silence hum and grow to a deadly edge –
but an unquiet love will stay quiet if kept
starving, choked, but fed just enough;
kept alive with dim, transient hopes.

Nullity

This single life. This life without a boy.
It equates to better skincare. I can be free
with the Nivea at night.
There's no-one to see. What a joy
it is, sliding between clean, unrumpled sheets,
Vaseline on lips, cocoa butter on hips and tits;
a greasy treasure trove;
the immaculate preservation of all my lovely bits.

I am a happy nullity under cold cotton covers;
this single life makes you too slippery for lovers.

Quietly Observing Him

I am raked in by a deepening,
a widening in my field of perception;
casting a gaze wider to catch you there, and I'm
suddenly receptive to the subtle balance
of blue and black in your hair.

Your quick-jointed, pointed step;
your unexpected dreams,
the deep way I want you,
present, to stay, to be there.

Blushing, ridiculous, I stare
quietly, here and there, when not noticed,
at the new possible familiar shape of your face.
Is it grace, or merely a tired heart that
wants to find peace there?

This Is Me For You

Tensile strength there is between us,
that kind of length, unwavering, deadly, strong to cross;
that thick wire they use on motorways to divide the
one way and the other way.

That you might cross it, but it would tear flesh:
a clean cut, or it might disfigure.
It might make us immobile if transgressed.

Like this, a fundamental deep seat,
this is me for you:
no clinging, no rough affection, no approximate smiles.
Me for you is bonded hard, steely,
irrevocable at the root and hard-lined,
no mess, no simper, no fuss,
but rightness, passion and strength binding the two of us.

Love Is Suffering's Reward

I want to write you a real cry,
a lunge; I want to rip my heart open and let you lick
the wound clean with a rough tongue –

now we have healed enough from being young,
midpoint, midheaven, possessed of
a wonderful jealous obsession;

I, queenly, regal, with the power to kill,
with the power of lustful evocation,
and us with death and the lessons of death in both our hearts still:
knowing tears and loneliness, knowing decay,
I want to love you hieroglyphically, indecipherable to others.

I want to write you a screaming, rebel cry:
spread my evangelical heart under your scrupulous eye.

But, beauty; harmony; care.
I want also to write you that, to give you
the soft satisfaction, the lips of the faithful . . . there . . . and there.

I insist that you reign from an impassive granite throne,
tended to, fed, watered, adored: never left alone;
that your praise will be unwavering,
the worshipful like petals under your heel.

My breath – idolatrous prayers on your shoulder at night,
my eyes, my arms, my fiery attentions holding you tight.

Healing

Change, be alive, push a heat ripple before you.
Breathe in pain and breathe out clearness, your old love shadows.

Merge into your cleansing, when structures momentarily melt.
You see the light mesh, the pattern that is air and not-air.

More than this: the universe breathes you out and in,
the connectedness, like a rough weave of linen,

through and around, fat and deep, punctuating you at light-level,
shades of sea-light in your face, making you shine, making you
  beautiful.

Making Potions

Making potions, making medicines,
seeing you laugh from afar,
I shuffle and chant for old miseries behind glass jars.

Day-sea greens refracting, constant in the salt air.
Through them, the health of your too-big blue eyes fail,
and peacock tails warn of the blue crab-eye means.

You say, join me in the green, the stalks still touching the earth;
leave your preserving, leave your dried revenges.

Mythologies

So it will come to pass:
the day when Carrie Bradshaw sleeps, and keeps
her maws in a glass.

By the bed flickers a TV séance
neurolinguistic programmers romance
blind, bound acetylene ladies:
salmon twinsets in community centres.

A roughly elevated Madonna with bouffant locks
wheeled over the cobbled blocks
by a shock of loose-limbed boys
glints past the devil, past the icons of today.

They cry, 'I prophesy, I prophesy
the new world will surge towards greatness,'
where prophecy, mystery, is baseless.

Yesodic

When I look at the letters in your name,
personality stripped back
to bare consonants and vowels,
how can you be called so, referred so,
when your name is such
a wider blue and orange shape –
something I hold in my mouth in dreams
but never grasp when awake?

It won't fly on lines on a page:
your trueness, the element of your being.
Only felt, like mango and blue suede.

Your name is only in Yesodic territory,
in the ether between form and love,
in the dinginess, where I once
formed you of clay with my sad hands;
where we once slept, and
where all the shells and cast-off skins are kept.

Between Boaz and Joachim

Black Omnia; the world in a seed.
A lonely Queen, there is nothing but
her, no noise, nothing of the senses.
A blank, starved, sated, open width.

The cold kiss of night sand between Boaz and Joachim.

Spaceless but for sentinels ruled by a lesser god,
where devotional cups hold moon-cups for tears and blood.

Hands on the holy book, mouthing sacred names,
pushing out the corners of a vacuum, repeating days,
repeating nights and twilights, the dark half of yang;
she holds a pure, sterile court. She holds force:
the point of stillness, the stillness of form.

O Beautiful Lord

O beautiful Lord,
thank you for this blue world,
the glass stars and the shiny mechanics,
the push-pull of the universe.
the turnover, knead and plough
of my energy, and the breath of my body.

O magnificent Lord, to you
I tread golden lotuses; so light,
I must be at Jerusalem,
uncrushed by the weight of glory.

O glorious, crownéd Lord,
when there is no succour,
when there are no juices of sustenance,
be the quenched throat in the desert when I sing my song,
and I will rise, rise on the dead night air,
your breath sounding in me,
pealing bells, summoning rain.

Turkish Bath

Steaminess is newly appreciated,
resting a foot on your jelly-under-velvet skin,
letting the old go, the salt run out,
lying in soapsuds, breathing you in.

Silky purdah, with
thin calves against plump brown thighs.
Remember where Sapphists glowed on blood-warm marble,
    and sigh;
monumental, but history
million-translated and declaimed, declawed:
sisterhood is not what it used to be.
Mourn, for Cybele rules no more.
Where dust reigns, only hope remains.

Aphrodite

The old forms are still there, but look closely.
Aphrodite, cast in plaster and gold leaf
lies on a dusty backroom shelf
in a back-country store.

Born from waves; whisper
a prayer in her shell-like. She will hear
though ears on Olympus are not what they were.
Currency is slack; the sapphire-robed lady walks
unattended in empty stone halls.

Yet the hazed horizon still speaks strong blue tones
and in it she can still appear, sea-crowned
with pearls and pink-lipped conchshells;
sweeping waves steadily, hush, hush,
shushing the lulling droves at the shore.

The forms will re-crystallise, given the proper awe.
The old ones still drift
on etheric ships, deep in Jungian groves.

Sea Mysteries

Come to her when the moon is full;
raise hands higher, chant undine lore,
toes in wet sand grip the sea floor.
Salt spray leaves diamonds in its place,
waves mask your land legs
and the sea wears her pretty face
as she caresses the rocks with her long loving fingers.

Over mysteries her depth lingers,
masking somnolent worlds.

Quiet now the songs at the sucking mouths of caves;
lost melodies roll under the waves.
Lighthouse eyes at the shore flicker
with an intoxicated, landlocked call:
the roiling, bitter, black and boundless sea
Stella Maris, Isis, Astarte; one and all,
walk over the waves, answer, appear!
Lady of the velvet, blue-black tides:
the jewel of the full moon is here.

Count the days back to the dawn of time –
invoke her name, voices carry behind the veil,
when all is still as the sterile lake and
the white womb in the dark before the light came;
lady of death in life and life in death,
we implore you, speak your Holy name!
Thousand-jewelled mistress of the stars:
on moon-bright tides lunar light shines
soft on the circle of flames.

Dream

Lost, humming a one-note harmony,
the half-world rotating, and you
floating along with it;

in an embryonic murk, milky comfort
mixes blue mist, and a threadbare veil
flutters, opaque on the shutters,
caught by a sultry breeze;
lazily repeating the lullaby of childhood:

sleep, sleep and dream.

Now the blue tip of the hummingbird wing,
now the deep, quick flying dips, soaring,
gasping across sunset hills;

pink chalk pavestones crumble
in the heat of lemon-picking time;
the musky, oily smell of vines –

you remember, you remember.

But now, glittering and black, the veil conceals
as if through tears a door
to indefinite dark corners:
low places, broken porcelain doll faces,
ju-ju in bags hermetically sealed.

The grey hag behind the counter shakes her bones,
casts them, laughs and wheezes;
in your palm are two bloodstones –
(dreamy, you ask,
'Do they portend well, please?') –
their sharp edges
bite ridges in your hands.

The crone whispers, 'My child –
your tears shall grow as salt statues
blown away by hot desert winds.'

Good Faith

I've often thanked God for you,
thanked the universe for your being,
thanked Him for the particular denseness of your belief in me,
your lifting of my spirits, believing,
exuding pure motivation, an engine
primed with good faith, inspiration, and
owning the secret password to the stars.

Artist

The otherness of being an artist. The strict
air-diet of trueness,
the liability to your muse,
straining to hear its call, its select words on the wing,
or securely attached to the earth,
its pull to the core,
to see the truth of things.

Networking

All it took was one open eye
strobing the Atlantic, and one fertile
Venus-girdled mind to house that gaze firmly, and plant it hard.

On contact, perspex ladders, grids and matrices formed from the
ocean, crossed land in vast bridges and
railed our talk back and forth,
a covert mirror mask,
almost undetectable, a glassy sheen,
gleaming, fast with secrets.

You know me by these networks;
you shall know me by my works.
My deepest red, made rose, carried to you by words
that phase lightly in time zones
foreign to me and comprised of all the sea salt in between.

We merge at a midpoint horizon, at tropics seen only in the mind's eye,
and you hum and haze, broadly material,
singing always of glorious reconciliation.

The Doctor

I have medicines to work with bodies and medicines to work with
    minds.
I run treadmills to the ocean,
heavy breakbeats to the breaking waves;
salt up my nose,
blue everywhere; big blue,
deep blue air.

Gulls singing, ongoing, reassuring
the ring of health only I can hear
clear and deep in my bones.

Silk light haze streams out of my hands,
healing hands,
arcs as I run, floating the breeze;
the lilac, grey-blue air
blowing through my molecules, my denseness and light.

Patchwork and Hope

She faced her lot with nothing but patchwork and hope,
hope in her hands.
I felt her pulling away
on elastic, on threads in the ether, in the ozone,
webs between her and me, hidden and
only sometimes a brief zazz in the light.
There is nothing you can do, except
wait, and test the web:
smile when it snaps back hard.

Visionary

You want to be visionary,
you want to kick the system;
still, with diamond skies,
Goa-blue skies that bounce off tiled roofs,
normal life still bites where it touches,
O magnificent raven one with songs made of clouds,
high, safe in your sanctuary.

Fairylight

It's what they used to call dusk,
The time when you imagine paperboys call and echo in a sepia tone.

Perhaps it's twilight, like with
Rose-red and the bear, or Beauty and the Beast.
The white roses shone at twilight, before the beast's roar.

And maybe it's just darkness, with the
mechanicality of tin men climbing the last steps home into the
    porch light.
When the street isn't lit, and Beauty lurks with her silver scissors
to snip at them if they step out of it.

It Was Nearly a Baby

Stand at the apex of the universe – your universe,
where your spark once stood, casting bones:
five layers in, your curse kicks you with febrile feet.

Chaos, in the cloak of creation, tumbles from race memory;
a malicious conjuror presses you close, to dance,
toes forced to grip the edge, the precipice
on the eve of your divorce.

As murky sea-clouds thronged Vesuvius when
she desperately spat out clay,
fine, quantum particles swirl and mummify you,
hold you fixed, desperate to flee, to separate:
to leave the sudden collapsing horror of Pompeii.

Now you stand, bowed, misaligned,
with your fraudulent, benign almost-child
raking dirty nails over your meridians.
Hoping for healing, that old velvet haze that used to fill your dreams
and beckon to your washed-in, wet grey-cotton days.

Jeans for Thoughtful Girls

When you sell jeans to thoughtful girls,
half-faced girls, with one half facing in;
you have to sell them salvation,
largesse and sex, right there on the tin.
By wearing them, somehow she will morph
into a Norse lust goddess, lithe with diamondsy bling.

She will walk with a feline drop-jawed slink,
past a line of officers and gentlemen, ready to hand-launder
her knickers, trimmed in mink.

Creatrix

Mammoth bones, did I form you?
Did I put you in the ground?
Like Alice, have I dreamt you?
When waves broke on Land's End
did I push the swell, and
did I cleave the cliff?

Did I create the world, code it and pack it?
Did I contemplate the unreality of the thumb,
a one-eyed dinosaur neck,
almost extinct, lonely on its own, but
opposed, and making the L in the hand, stand up?

Did I crack the cranium of early man and
store his remains in the strata for you to find?

If I see it first and name it, is it mine?

Then I am the explorer of my own land:
rare and savage, with
scars of discovery already planned in my heart.

Quiet

Don't wake anyone; do not disturb.
Vibrate the low notes, the
quiet, wrenching notes,
the tones right, right down at the dirgy bottom of the gut.

Pull the world over your head and sleep,
as if it were raw chicken skin,
easily separated from the whole,
skinned like a bunny
with Africa covering you;
funny, sad face and all.

It's War

I know slow emotional torture, and
gone is the sanctuary of believing that
a death camp is a sausage factory.

I know shady remorse and the stark end of
death on the never-never.

Away, in a sea of dust
when even fear is in the past:

Hope is one very small jewel,
one faraway star,
one cold tear on night-cream.

If Words Were Paint

If words were paint, I'd faint
over my wares.
To think, I could earn thousands
for hanging, quiet, on the stairs.

China Doll

Disturbed earth, topsoil to the left;
a blue crow hopped over and back.
Slick, black, it reverenced the earth.

Hack, hack; the spade on flinty ground. Hack.

All the laughs of a child's life fled –
a porcelain doll, a black matinée jacket,
shoved, forgotten, under the bed.
Painted chapped lips and moulded hair;

I shattered the crushed doll in the empty hole,
eggshells breaking and a misty blue crying-sigh:
'There,' it reassured. 'There, there.'

We Are Innocents

How new we are: let's not kid around.
Adolescents who bind and shelve what little wisdom, what little
antiquity precedes us;

still explorers, we are the first to
see jukebox jellyfish illume the depths,
where only a lighted lure in the dim is sure.

We are constant innovators.
Only a score of souls ago, Velasquez
honed the heart of Christ,
and far less back,
Grandfather gave the Nazis the sack.

Such innocents, we cultural adolescents.
We remember Plato, but
memory is the sugar glaze of history.

How new we are, us sparks, us bundles of baby id.

Clear the wadding from our soul receivers:
we are still unknowing;
we are still unbelievers.

Unseasonal

Strange birthdays, flitting by in shadow
sandwiched between a gaping smile,
doped movements, strange fruit, unseasonal.
Ripe, bluish, bruised, falling and rotting,
while a cheap digital clock
marks time with shallow, fighting breaths.

Audaciously white-coated,
he once roamed halls with purpose,
tapping a clipboard, and an assistant's
full, round, studious bottom;
to once have been reflected in his own
sterile, mechanical steel surfaces,
science poised for his pleasure,
pliant as a trained pup in his hand:

and to have come to this place.

I know the past by heart, but the present possesses
the eye: this vision
this slow-neuroned bag of shambling bones:

and there was never any other.

Soft Roads Lead Home

Soft roads lead home
to hot, tramped red earth,
blood clay earth, hard and cracked
crumbles in meringues, as chalk underfoot.

Slow glow red at midnight
above lowing farmtop roofs,
old doors, oak beams seen on night drives.

Wild eyes, reflecting, eerie, while
quietly glide the low-thrumming song of winding roads
leading you home.

Vanda

Diamond-headed with a square chin,
sallow, yellow
like a stunned snake
with dissociated block feet on skinny blue legs.

To the harsh rhythm of rails, she
smiles on, smiles on secretly,
emaciated with satisfaction.

Sitwellian Ego Dramas

To a Sitwellian
revenge is a hungry bird
and rips organs to shreds.

Not the liver, though.
Sitwellians prefer the heart instead.

Tears Will Get You in the End

Tears held in the body,
in the spine, for years
become black clumps
when the back slumps, crumps,
starts to chalkify, to calcify,
to turn renegade, refuse to mend;
have no doubt, my darling:
tears will get you in the end.

Teignmouth

We called it Timmouth.
We raced half-hearted snails,
coats on, hunkered on the tide wall.

We tried to have fun in the Wimpy.
She bought me pink candy-stripe shoes.
It didn't help at all.

The mechanic took us to a pub.
I wouldn't smile at the boy who
squealed in a wheelchair next to me
even though I should be kind,
even though we were on holiday, by the sea.

My time was at dusk
when fishermen's lamps glowed on night water,
with red crabnets and luminous jars of eels.

Outline

There is a line where a man could be.
A man-shaped line, an outline,
but not filled in, not completed.

The outline will do for now –
I'm loath to put on a beard or a bow tie yet.
The empty line is a much better bet.

Centre of the Line

Perfectly equatorial, between two poles,
a well-drawn India-inked path,
mapped by a spirit level.

The level of spirit thrumming
from the belly of a cello, deep and constant:
a long-vowelled lullaby.

Buddha-full, you benignly impart wisdom
whilst tapping ash neatly in a cup,
toes in the creamy shagpile.

A liner, cutting choppy water into safe, separate parts.

Body

If you didn't know better, you'd
imagine the brain was
floorless, wall-less, with sky-blue lightning flashes,
and we accessed it with an airy
embryonic cord, skinned to the scalp:
the grey jelly would be an eely, fishy lie.

And the body – a perfectly ordered but
mucus-lined floppy stack of meat.
An engine that periodically houses creation,
gestures, animated, then halts
and can be hung on a hook for all it cares.

If you didn't know better you'd forget the body,
rise unhindered and spread yourself thinly in
whatever airspace you can.

The Nucleus of Creation

Lips tingling against fast, jolting,
underlying rhythms
that jangle ceaselessly, discordant,
devised in foetal chaos,
steeped in mucus and green shoots – the rising sap,
baby brine, fecund like an itch in the throat.

Disorganised, falling, fucking head over arse,
nothing but life,
life is nothing but hot green pods
sticky with seeds,
while structures lift and fall and suggest a mendacious order.

Justine, Office Slut

Slipshod, she is. Bleary.
The shadow of pyjama stalks her lazy mien.
Heel-tips fall into cracked steps, with
the latest rag furled under her unfocused elbow.
With learned stealth, Justine fingers dirty upholstery:
belly slack, instinct absent,
mind card-filing desperate, seductive minutae.

In Response to a Piece of Performance Art

Your beauty was so high that I thought
I am a new being now. It reinvented me
by sight of perfection, by realisation, by epiphany.

My response is as organic as your blood-spattered silk jade robe and
your floured sweat, the light rises and ravines on your small, strong
  arms.

Confined by stretches, lifts, a quick wet cat, sashing the rope you
  hung on,
you were like a hard exhale, body force focused on a straight gaze.

You hung in the lights, caught, perfect, utterly weighted and
  capturing flow wordlessly.